POPULAR PIANO SOLOS

Pop Hits, Broadway, Movies and More!

ISBN 978-1-4234-0907-6

WILLIS MUSIC

EXCLUSIVELY DISTRIBUTED BY

7777 W. BLUEMOUND RD. P.O. BOX 13819 MILWAUKEE, WI 53213

Visit Hal Leonard Online at
www.halleonard.com

Contents

Till There Was You
from Meredith Willson's THE MUSIC MAN

Use with John Thompson's Modern Course for the Piano
FOURTH GRADE BOOK, after p. 15.

By Meredith Willson
Arranged by Glenda Austin

Moon River
from the Paramount Picture BREAKFAST AT TIFFANY'S

Use after page 19.

Words by Johnny Mercer
Music by Henry Mancini
Arranged by Glenda Austin

Expressively, not rushed

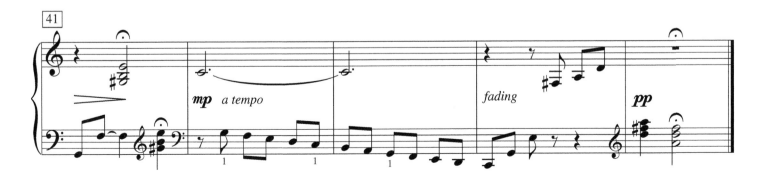

Imagine

Use after page 27.

Words and Music by John Lennon
Arranged by Glenda Austin

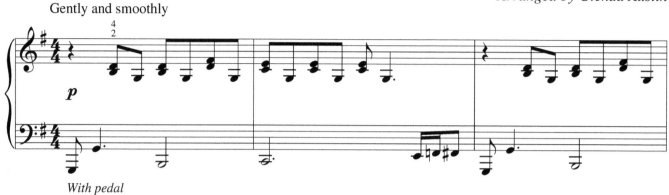

Somewhere Out There

from AN AMERICAN TAIL

Use after page 35.

Music by Barry Mann and James Horner
Lyric by Cynthia Weil
Arranged by Glenda Austin

12

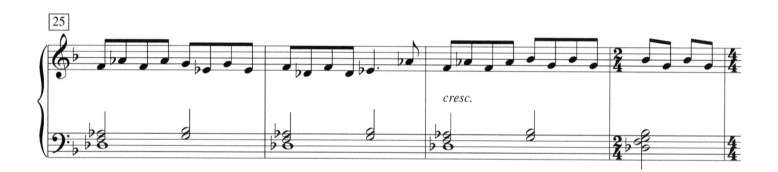

On Broadway

Use after page 43.

Words and Music by Barry Mann,
Cynthia Weil, Mike Stoller and Jerry Leiber
Arranged by Glenda Austin

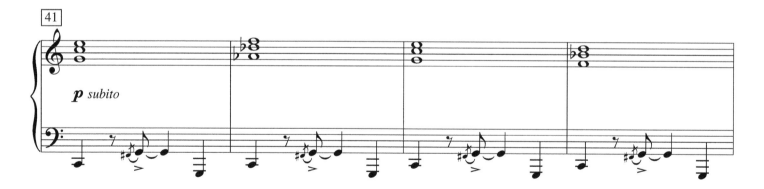

Chariots of Fire

Use after page 57.

Music by Vangelis
Arranged by Glenda Austin

Triumphantly, with a steady beat

With pedal

Endless Love

Use after page 71.

Words and Music by Lionel Richie
Arranged by Glenda Austin

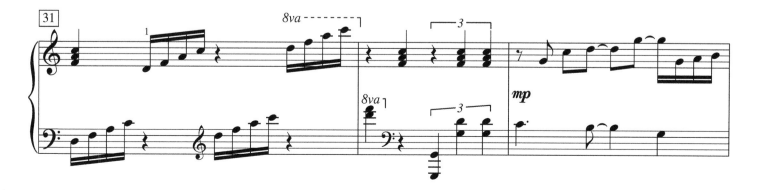

A Whole New World

from Walt Disney's ALADDIN

Use after page 83.

Music by Alan Menken
Lyrics by Tim Rice
Arranged by Glenda Austin

Not too fast, gently rhythmic

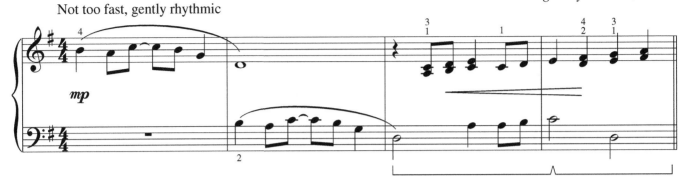

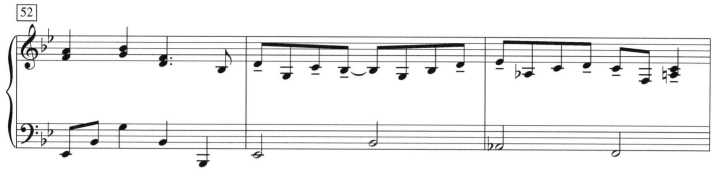

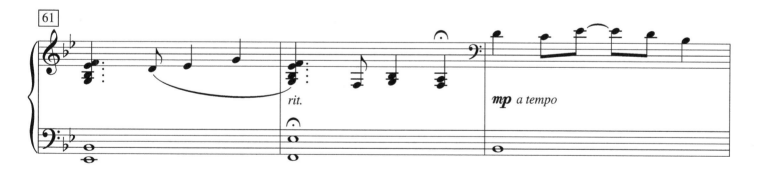

Mission: Impossible Theme

from the Paramount Television Series MISSION: IMPOSSIBLE

Use after page 92.

By Lalo Schifrin
Arranged by Glenda Austin

Accented, with drive

Seasons of Love

from RENT

Use after page 92.

Words and Music by Jonathan Larson
Arranged by Glenda Austin